LIVES OF IRISH ARTISTS

N. Hone

Nathaniel Hone the Elder
1718-1784

ADRIAN LE HARIVEL

N. Hone

Nathaniel Hone the Elder
1718 - 1784

ADRIAN LE HARIVEL

THE NATIONAL GALLERY OF IRELAND
IN ASSOCIATION WITH
TOWN HOUSE, DUBLIN

Published in 1992 by

Town House

42 Morehampton Road

Donnybrook

Dublin 4

for The National Gallery of Ireland

British Library Cataloguing in Publication Data

Harivel, Adrian Le

Nathaniel Hone the Elder, 1718–1784. —

(Lives of Irish Artists Series)

I. Title II. Series

759.2915

ISBN: 0-948524-36-7

Cover: *The Piping Boy* 1769 (NGI)

Title page: *Self-Portrait c* 1780 (NGI)

Managing editor: Treasa Coady

Series editor: Brian P Kennedy (NGI)

Text editors: Elaine Campion, Bernie Daly

Design concept: Q Design

Colour origination: The Kulor Centre

Printed in Hong Kong

CONTENTS

ILLUSTRATIONS

Adrian Le Harivel was born in Paris in 1957. He attended Westminster School in London, and gained his History of Art MA at Edinburgh University. Following a brief period at Dulwich Picture Gallery in London, he moved to Dublin, and has been a curator at the National Gallery of Ireland since 1981. He has a particular interest in all aspects of the arts in the eighteenth century and is currently researching the Gallery's collection of British paintings.

8

Nathaniel Hone the Elder is best known today for his satirical painting *The Conjuror*, which caused an uproar when he submitted it to the Royal Academy in 1775. In his lifetime, in spite of little formal training, he graduated from painting miniatures to establish himself as a leading portrait painter in London, and was a pioneer of a more sympathetic approach to child portraiture. Hone was an accomplished mezzotint (copper-plate) engraver, and over thirty of his pictures were engraved by himself and others. He assembled a noted collection of old master drawings, most of which were sold after his death. Two of his sons became well-known miniature painters, and both the nineteenth-century landscapist Nathaniel Hone the Younger and the twentieth-century stained-glass artist Evie Hone are his direct descendants.

In Pursuit of Fame

Nathaniel Hone the Elder was born in Dublin on 24 April 1718, one of five sons of a merchant living on Wood Quay. The family was Presbyterian, and had emigrated from Holland in the seventeenth century. Hone had little interest in business and, if not self-taught as an artist, may have studied with Robert West, who ran an art school in George's Lane. Moving to England, Hone became an itinerant portraitist, and in 1742 he married a young heiress, Mary Earle, at York Minster. She is thought to have been the illegitimate daughter of a noble, or 'some Lord's cast-off mistress' as she was later described. She brought Hone an income of £200 a year.

Anthony Pasquin, who disliked Hone, included a scurrilous biography of the artist in his *Artists of Ireland* (1796); he claimed that this 'erratic portrait painter' would choose the best hostelry in a town, and having asked to dine with the family, would praise the beauty of their children. He then ascertained if their portraits had been drawn, before offering his services: 'The portmanteau was unpacked, and the operations began; while the fond and partial parents hung in rapture over his shoulder.... Thus he made his establishment secure, and gave general satisfaction, by offending truth and outraging taste; making the children as angels, the mother as a Venus, and the husband a well-fed Job, in a brown perriwig!'

Little is actually known of Hone's early life. The earliest dated oil is 1741, but few works survive before the mid-1740s. To publicise his arrival in London, Hone engraved his 1748 portrait of Elisabetta Gambarini as the frontispiece to her *Lessons on the Harpsichord*. In a letter the same year, the adventuress Mrs Letitia Pilkington praised his ability to portray a strong likeness. She was later painted by Hone as a rather intimidating figure, and the image was used as a frontispiece to her husband's biography. A miniature of the *3rd Earl of Essex* (National Gallery of Ireland), and a pastel, *Man in a Brown Coat* (NGI), both from 1747, show Hone's early style, with oversized heads and stylised features. In 1752 Hone was living in Henrietta Street, London. He had nearly sixty sitters listed in his diary and was charging ten guineas for a miniature. His last miniatures date from the 1760s, when they show a more sophisticated rendering of features, greater realism and more detailed finish, as in *Unknown Lady* (*Pl 2*). Lace is often in opaque white, with a dotted technique or occasional hatching, as in his large miniature of *Edmund Burke* (NGI), to model faces and clothes.

It was once thought that Hone had visited Florence in 1752 because he became a member of the Florentine Academy in that year. In fact this was *11* arranged by his brother Samuel, a minor painter who later worked in Jamaica. In August 1753 Nathaniel Hone visited Paris for a month. On his return to London, his income from painting, business transactions, taking a lodger and even boarding his sister's child, allowed him to dress well, attend the theatre, masques, dances and fashionable gatherings at Ranelagh and Vauxhall, and he even began to collect the works of other artists. He advised the Princess of Wales on her collection, and increasing numbers of the nobility sat to him. Early life-size portraits such as *Viscount Milsington* (1753) share a smoothness of finish and easy naturalism with the young Thomas Gainsborough, and occasionally have been attributed to him. Hone's interest in Rembrandt is also seen in portraits such as *John Hinchcliffe* (*Pl 1*), where the head and (unfinished) hand holding a book are picked out by the lighting against a dark background. While his miniatures are invariably clearly signed with his monogram *NH*, his oils tend to have the monogram or his full signature *N Hone* only lightly scratched in the paint with the end of a brush, so that it is difficult to discern and has often been lost in later cleaning.

❧

EXHIBITIONS

By 1760 Hone clearly aspired to be taken more seriously as a painter and, as he later said, he 'gave up his leisure-hours from that time to paint in oil'. Established artists such as Thomas Hudson and Alan Ramsay were nearing the end of their careers and the next generation, including Hone, Thomas Gainsborough, Joshua Reynolds and Samuel Cotes, were coming to the fore. Hone sent *A Brickdust Man* to the first exhibition of the Society of Artists in 1760. This was the first showing in London of what became known as a 'fancy piece' subject, and a mezzotint of it was engraved by the Irishman James Watson. The range of Hone's exhibits up to 1768 suggests that patronage was uneven: portrait miniatures and a fly in enamel in 1761; one of his two majestic portraits of blind magistrate *Sir John Fielding* (National Portrait Gallery, London) in 1762; *Kitty Fisher* (*Pl 5*) in 1765; *Diogenes Looking for an*

cont. p25

ILLUSTRATIONS

PLATE 1

John Hinchcliffe 1757

Pl 1   John Hinchcliffe (1731–1794), painted the year he received his MA, was later headmaster of his old school Westminster, Vice-chancellor of Cambridge University, and from 1769 Bishop of Peterborough. Hone is not yet fully confident in full-size portraiture, but he responds to an attractive face, and includes the mortarboard to give a jaunty aspect.

Oil on canvas; 74.5 x 61.5 cm
National Portrait Gallery, London

PLATE 2

Unknown Lady 1760
Sir Henry St John, Bt 1763

14

Pl 2 Hone was a master of both watercolour and enamel
miniature painting, as these examples show. Though
small in size, they include all the detail of fashionable
clothes, hair and ornaments. The unknown lady, painted
in watercolour, contrasts with the bright enamel colours
fixed by firing, in the portrait of Sir Henry St John. Hone
signed both with his monogram NH.

Watercolour on ivory; 3.65 x 3.2 cm
Victoria and Albert Museum, London

Enamel on gold; 3.4 x 2.8 cm
National Gallery of Ireland

PLATE 3

Captain The Hon. Boyle Walsingham 1760

Pl 3   T*his portrait commemorates the captain's participation in the British capture of the French naval base at Louisburgh, Nova Scotia, in 1758. His ship was part of the naval blockade, while the Army, under General Wolfe, captured and razed the newly built fortress. The captain is stiffly posed but memorable for his engaging face and the exactitude of costume detail.*

Oil on canvas; 239 x 145 cm
On loan to Castletown House, Co. Kildare

Pl 4   N*athaniel Curzon, first Baron Scarsdale (1727-1804), of Kedleston, Derbyshire, married Lady Caroline Colyear (1733-1812), eldest daughter of the second Earl of Portmore, in 1750. Hone painted her miniature in 1752 and created this double portrait masterpiece in 1761. They are shown promenading in the grounds of a house representing Kedleston (then being rebuilt by Robert Adam).*

Oil on canvas; 264 x 182 cm
Kedleston Hall (National Trust)

16

N. Hone

PLATE 4

Baron and Baroness Scarsdale 1761

17

LORD & LADY SCARSDALE
1761

PLATE 5

Kitty Fisher 1765

18

Catherine (Kitty) Fisher (d 1767) *had become a well-known London beauty and courtesan by 1760 when she advertised to complain of abuse in newspapers, claiming that she was 'exposed in the print shops'. Reynolds painted her several times, most notably as Cleopatra, and this was surely Hone's riposte, exhibited at the Society of Artists in 1765. The seemingly demure figure conceals her charms with an embroidered fichu and is wittily identified by a kitten trying to get into a basin of gold fish (kitty fisher).*

19

Oil on canvas; 74.9 x 62.2 cm
National Portrait Gallery, London

PLATE 6

Horace Hone Drawing a Cast *c* 1766

Pl 6   **H**orace Hone (1756–1825) was the artist's second son and later an accomplished miniature painter, working in both Dublin and London. Mental illness from around 1807 ended his career. In this charming subject picture, he pauses while drawing a cast of the head of the Venus de' Medici, one of the most celebrated antique statues of Venus, and a typical exercise for artists.

Oil on canvas; 128 x 105 cm
National Gallery of Ireland

20

PLATE 7

The Piping Boy 1769

21

Pl 7   **R**esponding to the public's liking for idealised children's portraits, Hone exhibited this picture of his son John Camillus (1759-1836) as a shepherd boy, at the 1769 Royal Academy. His inspiration was probably A Boy with a Pipe in the Royal Collection, an idyllic pastoral figure, then attributed to the Venetian artist Giorgione. John Camillus was later a painter and worked principally in Calcutta and Dublin.

Oil on canvas; 36 x 31 cm
National Gallery of Ireland

PLATE 8

Self-Portrait *c* 1760

Pl 8   A*mong Hone's numerous self-portraits this is one of the most vivid, as he regards us half-smiling, a folio under his arm and a holder with red chalk in his hand. The scumbled paint of the face and its red highlights provide a foil for the rich blue velvet coat and open collar of his shirt.*

22

Oil on canvas; 74.9 x 61 cm
National Portrait Gallery, London

PLATE 9

The Conjuror 1775

23

Pl 9   T*he most famous of Hone's pictures was refused admission to the 1775 Royal Academy Exhibition. The artist Angelica Kauffmann had objected that she was depicted as a nude caricature in the distance (Hone painted this out), but it was clearly understood that his real attack was on Sir Joshua Reynolds 'to charge with plagiarism the first portrait painter perhaps this country ever produced'. The aged conjuror represents Reynolds, who transforms the Italian and Flemish old master prints into a picture (while holding a print in which time reveals truth).*

Oil on canvas; 145 x 173 cm
National Gallery of Ireland

PLATE 10

The Hon. Mrs Nathaniel Curzon 1778

24

Pl 10 Sophia Susanna Noel (1758-1782) was the third daughter of Viscount Wentworth and was painted after her marriage to Nathaniel Curzon, later second Baron Scarsdale. This is one of Hone's noblest portraits. There is a Roman gravity in the restrained demeanour, timeless dress and veil-like scarf. With the air of a muse, she rests a music scroll against an ornamented pedestal.

Oil on canvas; 126.7 x 100.3 cm
Fitzwilliam Museum, Cambridge

cont. from p12

Honest Man and *Rev George Whitfield* in 1768. Hone did not gain significant church patronage, but he painted several popular preachers, including John Wesley (National Portrait Gallery, London). His full-length portraits often lacked the suave assurance of rivals (as in *Pl 3*), and one of his masterpieces, *Baron and Baroness Scarsdale (Pl 4)*, may never have been shown in London. This painting was one of six bought by the Curzon family over three decades, most of which are still at Kedleston Hall in Derbyshire. *The Hon. Juliana Curzon* (1776) shows Baron Scarsdale's daughter with her dog against a bridge, while the second baron's wife *The Hon. Mrs Nathaniel Curzon* of 1778 (*Pl 10*) was a more formal composition and almost the only time that Hone included references to classical antiquity in a portrait.

25

In 1766 Hone became one of the directors of the Society of Incorporated Artists of Great Britain, but he left in 1768 with other artists to become a founder member of the Royal Academy. He exhibited sixty-nine works at the Academy up to the time of his death in 1784. For the inaugural 1769 Royal Academy exhibition, he rightly judged that *The Piping Boy (Pl 7)* would attract attention. This picture shows him at his most Italianate, reworking the composition of a prized painting bought by Charles I for the Royal Collection. In general, Hone followed in the sway of Hogarth and the Anglo-Dutch tradition of truth to nature, standing out against the general trend. Some found his manner raw and lacking in taste, probably as a result of his painting *Two Gentlemen in Masquerade* (RA, 1770), an extraordinary double portrait of his friends Francis Grose and Theodosius Forrest as Capuchin friars feasting at a table. Forrest was originally shown stirring a bowl of punch with a crucifix, but Hone was requested by the Royal Academy to replace this with a ladle. Two years later he both engraved and published a mezzotint of it with the crucifix, and he exhibited the picture in its original form in his 1775 one-man exhibition. From 1771 Hone mainly exhibited portraits: a large number of children and of unidentified adults.

❧

SELF-PORTRAITS

Hone painted at least eight oil and two miniature portraits of himself, and they serve as an interesting record of the image he wished to project. Their number has been put down to 'inordinate vanity' or his love of playing a role, and some certainly do have a theatrical quality as they show off his broad, noble features. From the start he shows his admiration for Rembrandt, as in his engraved 1747 *Self-Portrait*, where he is seen wearing a fur cap, dramatically lit against a plain background, using shadow to compensate for his weak draughtsmanship. Reynolds was also experimenting with similar lighting effects at this date and both artists demonstrate the great interest in Rembrandt at that time.

Hone's early *Self-Portrait* (NGI), in which he is seen leaning on a folio, engraved probably in the late 1750s, is a traditional representation of an artist, chalk in hand and ready for his next client. The engaging tilt of his head only serves to emphasise its block-like quality. An oversized head is again a feature of an enamel miniature *Self-Portrait* of about 1750 (National Portrait Gallery, London). In the 1760s Hone presented himself with greater assurance: actually working (*Pl 8*) or, in the *Self-Portrait* (NGI), posing, palette in hand (but over-dressed for the studio), and gesturing towards a portrait of his wife Mary which he painted in 1760. Rembrandt again inspired a *Self-Portrait* of about 1765 (Royal Academy, London), a 'costume piece' with lace collar and wide-brimmed hat, which casts a deep shadow over the left side of his face. There is a glamourised *Self-Portrait* of 1778 (Manchester City Art Gallery), again with shadows thrown by a hat, which perfectly matches J T Smith's description of Hone in his *Life of Nollekens* as a 'tall, upright, large man, with a broad-rimmed hat and a lapelled coat buttoned up to his stock'. Hone inscribed the picture as painted at Petworth, which was the Sussex home of the third Earl of Egremont, later friend and patron of Turner. Hone presented himself as a country gentleman, an image reinforced in his late *Self-Portrait* of about 1780 (frontispiece). Here he pauses while on a walk with his dog, and rests himself on a sculpted relief. While the distant temple clearly derives from the famed Temple of Vesta at Tivoli, it also suggests a feature in an English landscaped garden such as Stourhead. What appears to be a Roman relief is actually a portrait of his wife. Hone's pose is strangely anticipated in Zoffany's 1771–72 group portrait *The Academicians of the Royal Academy* (Royal Collection), where Hone is seen in profile stretching out his hand over a folio. In his *Self-Portrait* of 1780, Hone's face is as lined as a late Rembrandt, but his expression remains optimistic and, as in all his self-portraits, there is none of Rembrandt's introspection, but rather the sense of a man of the world, not always identifiable as an artist, which is very unusual in eighteenth-century self-portraits.

***

CHILDREN'S PORTRAITS

Hone and his wife Mary had five sons and five daughters, though Samuel, Apelles, Lydia, Sophia and

Floreth all died young. Hone clearly enjoyed being with children and painted them sympathetically, but he was not averse to exploiting his own family as material for genre subjects. John Camillus (1745-1836) sat for *The Piping Boy* (*Pl 7*), engraved by Hone's friend, the amateur engraver William Baillie, in 1771, and for *A Boy Deliberating on his Drawing* (Ulster Museum), which may be the picture exhibited at the Society of Artists in 1766. He was also *The Spartan Boy* (RA, 1775), where a boy conceals a fox in his garment and suffers a mortal bite rather than reveal it to pursuers. Horace Hone (1756-1825) was shown drawing a cast (*Pl 6*) and, like his brother, protecting an animal in *David the Shepherd Boy* (1771). Lydia Hone (1760-1775), who died of consumption in her teens, was painted as a young girl holding a white rabbit which she has saved from a fox, and as Shakespeare's Juliet, both engraved 1771. The same year, Amelia Hone, later Mrs Ambrose Rigg, modelled for one of her father's most stylish pictures, in which she is seen taking tea, a composition clearly inspired by a French painter such as Chardin or Lancret. Like Rembrandt, Hone even painted his elderly mother (RA, 1771). His son Nathaniel, who became a captain in the Wiltshire Militia, was not painted by him.

It becomes difficult to separate the children's portraits painted after the late 1760s, from Hone's genre paintings. In *George Douglas, later 16th Earl of Morton and his Brother* (1769), also called *The Bird Nesters*, a bird and its nest provide the subject matter, as does the garland of flowers held by Master Muspratt Williams in *A Boy Composing a Garland* (RA, 1771), while *Miss Metcalfe with a Pomeranian Dog* (engraved 1772) refers to his granddaughter's rescue by her dog from a fire in Rome. Many of his pictures of children are only known by popular titles such as *Boy with a Pitcher*, *The Student* or *The Green Boy* (1782). They typically have rather glazed expressions, with bright faces, red lips, and strong highlights in the eyes. Hone's blend of innocent charm and sweetness is at times a little cloying, but his affinity for children often captures the wistful transiency of childhood, surpassed only by Gainsborough. His directness anticipates the next generation of George Romney and Thomas Lawrence. In comparison, however animated, the children painted by William Hogarth and Alan Ramsay before him, still seem part of a formal adult world.

30

ॐ

THE CONJUROR

Hone was known for his quick temper and ambitious nature. He held an especially strong antagonism for Sir Joshua Reynolds, elected first president of the Royal Academy and judged the preeminent painter of the day. In 1774 Reynolds' topic for his annual *Discourse* lecture, given at the prizegiving for students, was the judicious copying by artists from their predecessors. He acknowledged the danger of plagiarism. This may have inspired Hone to paint his best-known work *The Conjuror* (*Pl 9*), where the sources of numerous Reynolds pictures are revealed. His full title for it was *The Pictorial Conjuror, Displaying the Whole Art of Optical Deception*. The picture was initially accepted for the 1775 Royal Academy exhibition, but according to Hone, was declined after it had hung for several days because 'it had been rumoured that he had made an indecent figure or caricature of an eminent female artist'. This was Angelica Kauffmann, leading female portrait and mythological painter and close friend of Sir Joshua Reynolds. Her particular objection was to the seated figure with an ear-trumpet. Hone denied that the figure in question represented her, but he painted it over with artists at a table. The original figure is seen now only in Hone's sketch (Tate Gallery, London). Hone later announced that he was exhibiting the picture, with 'upwards of fourscore Pictures, both large and small, painted by his own hands' and, hiring a room at 70 St Martin's Lane, opposite Old Slaughters Coffee House, proceeded to

31

hold the first one-man exhibition in Britain. The catalogue contained his defence of *The Conjuror*. There were sixty-six exhibits in all: oil portraits, enamel miniatures, landscapes and subject pictures.

❧

THE LATER YEARS

Hone continued to exhibit at the Royal Academy after 1775. He took an apartment in Schomberg House, Pall Mall, where Irish painter Charles Jervas had earlier lived, though the house is now most associated with Thomas Gainsborough. Hone was later said to have 'kept a famous black woman...as his model'. There is a dignified restraint in Hone's finest late portraits, such as *The Misses Knight* (1775), *The Hon. Mrs Nathaniel Curzon* (*Pl 10*), or his *Self-Portrait* (frontispiece). He continued with half-lengths such as the 1776 pendants of *Benjamin Cole* and *Mrs Benjamin Cole* (Yale Center for British Art, New Haven), or the *Portrait of a Man* of 1781 (NGI), and the probable portrait of printseller *Nathaniel Smith* from 1784 (NGI). In a rare military double portrait of *Lt-General The Hon. Philip Sherard and Captain Tiffin* (1782), the composition has advanced little since the 1760s (see *Pl 3*). It was left to the extended caption on the 1782 engraving to explain that the officers were relieving a position during the battle of Bruckenmühle.

Hone was a keen art collector but no catalogue of his collection was ever made. *The Angel Departing from Tobit and his Family* was probably his finest picture. Then thought to be by Rembrandt, and engraved as such in 1765, it is now known to be a version of the picture in the Louvre. His drawings collection, with his collector's mark of a human eye, is now dispersed. There is a volume of Fra Bartolommeo studies in the British Museum, and a few drawings in the National Gallery of Ireland, bequeathed by Eleanor Hone in 1912. They are mainly seventeenth-century works, the finest a small *St Mary Magdalen* by Guercino.

Hone died at 44 Rathbone Place, London, on 14 August 1784, and was buried in the family plot at Hendon churchyard. Hone's studio contents were sold on 2 and 3 March 1785, and while the first day consisted of twenty-two mixed pictures and forty-three miniatures, no catalogue has survived for the second. J T Smith reported that he 'saw Sir Joshua Reynolds most attentively view the picture of the Conjuror for full ten minutes'.

Hone is justly admired today for the immediacy and sparkle of his society portraits, also for his enchanting images of children. An irascible personality hindered his career and, consequently, he did not receive due credit for his 'fancy pictures' and for his intuitive response to sitters. Hone's defiant retrospective exhibition in 1775, which confronted the British art establishment, is now seen as a key event in the development of the status of artists.